WATER

WHY WE DRINK TO REFUEL

FUEL Up!

by Harriet Brundle

BEARPORT
PUBLISHING

Minneapolis, Minnesota

Credits: :
Cover & Throughout - Rhenzy, notkoo, zsooofija, NotionPic, Littlekidmoment, Liderina, 2&3 - Irina Danyliuk, Victoruler, Inspiring, 4&5 - peiyang, Robert Kneschke, 6&7 - 3445128471, 8&9 - Dave Pot, Sergey Melnikov, 10&11 - Africa Studio, NotionPic, 12&13 - ann131313, Yuri Shevtsov, 14&15 - KK Tan, Pixel-Shot, 16&17 - ann131313, kornnphoto, 18&19 - PJjaruwan, Valentyn Volkov, shuvector, 20&21 - Sunnydream, VikiVector, Iurii Kiliian, Colorcocktail, Anastasia Petrova, Sofija Djukic, Kataryna Lanskaya, Pond's Saksit, G-Stock Studio, 22&23 - ann131313, Andrii Bezvershenko, graphic-line.

Images are courtesy of Shutterstock.com. With thanks to Getty Images, Thinkstock Photo, and iStockphoto.

All facts, statistics, web addresses, and URLs in this book were verified as valid and accurate at time of writing. No responsibility for any changes to external websites or references can be accepted by either the author or publisher.

Library of Congress Cataloging-in-Publication Data

Names: Brundle, Harriet, author.
Title: Water : why we drink to refuel / by Harriet Brundle.
Description: Fusion. | Minneapolis : Bearport Publishing Company, [2021] | Series: Fuel up | Includes bibliographical references and index.
Identifiers: LCCN 2020009350 (print) | LCCN 2020009351 (ebook) | ISBN 9781647473464 (library binding) | ISBN 9781647473518 (paperback) | ISBN 9781647473563 (ebook)
Subjects: LCSH: Water in the body–Juvenile literature. | Drinking water–Juvenile literature.
Classification: LCC QP535.H1 .B78 2021 (print) | LCC QP535.H1 (ebook) | DDC 612/.01522–dc23
LC record available at https://lccn.loc.gov/2020009350
LC ebook record available at https://lccn.loc.gov/2020009351

For more information, write to Bearport Publishing, 5357 Penn Avenue South, Minneapolis, MN 55419. Printed in the United States of America.

CONTENTS

Water is one of the most important things on Earth. Every living thing needs water to stay alive.

WATER

Most people couldn't live for more than three or four days without water. The water we get from what we eat and drink **fuels** our bodies.

WHY DO I NEED WATER?

Water helps us pee and poop. It also helps make **saliva**. This keeps our mouths healthy and helps to break down the food we eat.

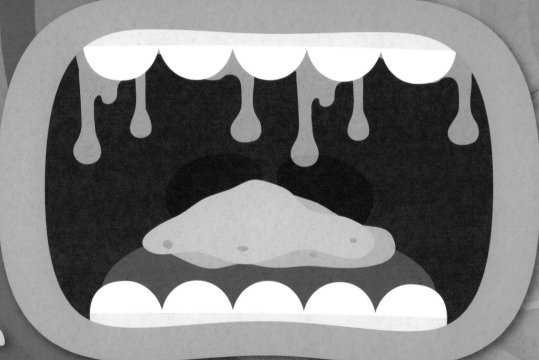

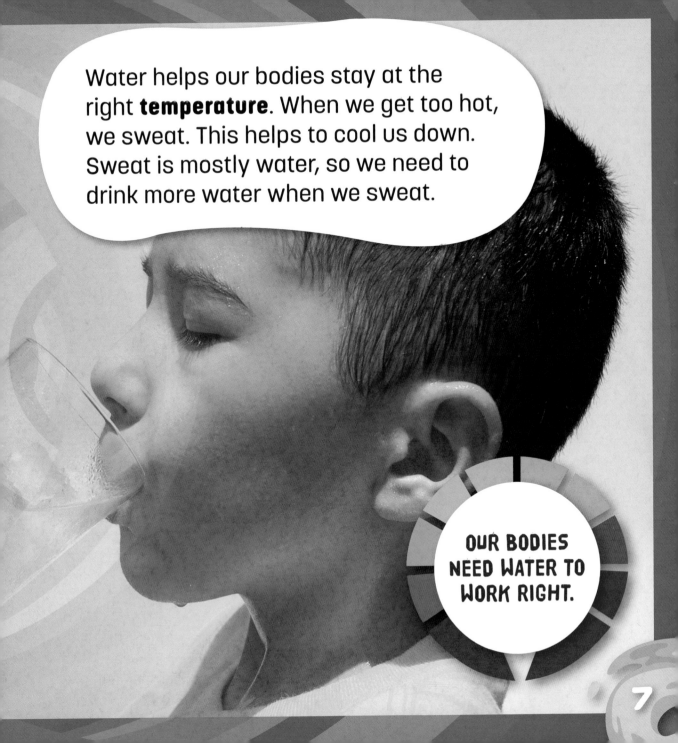

Water helps our bodies stay at the right **temperature**. When we get too hot, we sweat. This helps to cool us down. Sweat is mostly water, so we need to drink more water when we sweat.

OUR BODIES NEED WATER TO WORK RIGHT.

7

HOW MUCH DO I NEED?

Making sure you get enough water is very important. As you get older, you need to drink more water each day.

1 GLASS =
8.5 OUNCES
(250 MILLILITERS)

1–3 YEAR OLDS NEED 4 GLASSES EACH DAY

4–8 YEAR OLDS NEED 5 GLASSES EACH DAY

PEOPLE 9 YEARS AND OLDER NEED 6 GLASSES EACH DAY

You should drink water throughout the day, rather than all at once. Having a glass of water at every meal will help you get at least half of the water you need every day.

WHEN DO I NEED MORE?

There are times when we need to drink more water. You'll need to drink more if it's a hot day or if you've been getting exercise and sweating a lot.

If you've been sick, your body has lost **fluids**. You need to drink more water to put them back in your body.

11

NOT ENOUGH WATER

If you don't drink enough water, you might feel thirsty, dizzy, and tired.

WHEN YOU DON'T DRINK ENOUGH YOUR PEE LOOKS DARKER THAN USUAL.

Drinking water keeps you healthy. If you haven't had enough to drink, it's important to drink water right away.

13

HOW TO REHYDRATE

If you don't drink enough, you need to **rehydrate** as soon as possible. Try to take small sips of water very often.

TIPS FOR DRINKING WATER

If you find it hard to drink enough water, there are some things you can try. If you don't like plain water, add a slice of lemon or orange to it.

You can also use a water bottle with **measurements** on it that shows how much water you have had.

DRINK SOME WATER EVERY TIME YOU FEEL THIRSTY.

17

Some fruits, vegetables, and soups have lots of water. They will help you have enough water every day.

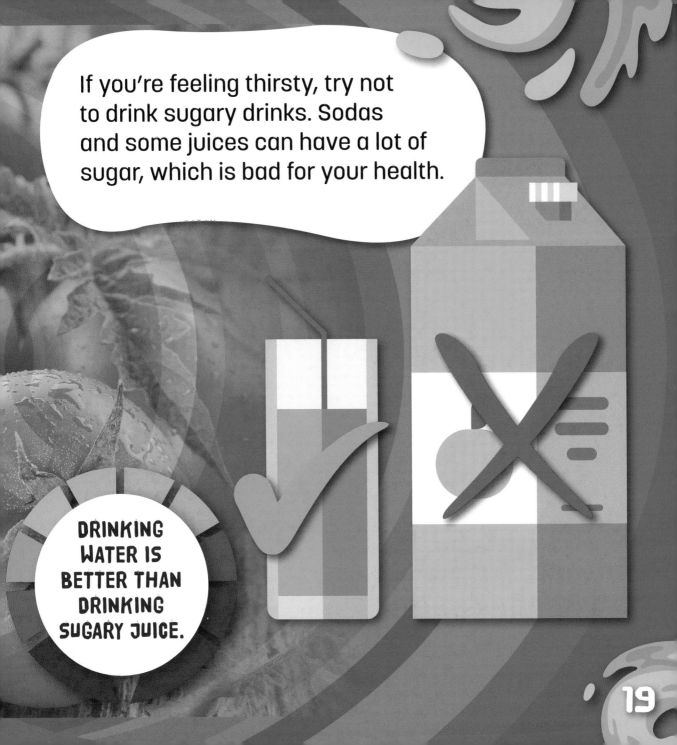

If you're feeling thirsty, try not to drink sugary drinks. Sodas and some juices can have a lot of sugar, which is bad for your health.

DRINKING WATER IS BETTER THAN DRINKING SUGARY JUICE.

A HEALTHY LIFESTYLE

Keeping our bodies fueled with plenty of water is important. So is eating a **balanced** diet from all the different food groups.

CARBS

DAIRY

PROTEIN

FRUITS AND VEGETABLES

It's important to get lots of exercise to keep your body healthy. Sleeping well will help you feel great, too!

Fuel Up with Water!

Think about how much water you drank today. Then, look at the image below. Have you had enough water today?

1 GLASS = 8.5 OZ (250 ML)

1–3 YEAR OLDS NEED 4 GLASSES EACH DAY

4–8 YEAR OLDS NEED 5 GLASSES EACH DAY

PEOPLE 9 YEARS AND OLDER NEED 6 GLASSES EACH DAY

Think about what you have eaten today. Have you had any foods with lots of water in them? How much exercise have you gotten? Have you done anything that might mean you need more water than usual?

23

GLOSSARY

balanced the right amount of things

fluids materials that flow, such as water

fuels gives energy or power to something

measurements the amounts of something

rehydrate drink to have enough water again

saliva the liquid made in the mouth to help with digestion and tasting

temperature how hot or cold something is

INDEX